I speak life into

_____

_____

_____

_____

In loving memory of my "earthly" father,
Elder Edward Buckner

O Lord, you have examined me, and you know me.
You alone know when I sit down and when I get up.
You read my thoughts from far away.

You watch me when I travel and when I rest.
You are familiar with all my ways.

Even before there is a single word on my tongue,
you know all about it, Lord.

You are all around me—in front of me and in back of me.
You lay your hand on me.

Such knowledge is beyond my grasp.
It is so high I cannot reach it.

Psalm 139:1-6

Copyright © 2015 by Terri Bell
Divinely Inspired Publications
109 Frasier Bay Road, Columbia, SC 29229
www.KingdomKidsBooks.com

All rights reserved. No part of this publication may be reproduced, distributed, or transmitted in any form or by any means, including photocopying, recording, or other electronic or mechanical methods, without the prior written permission of the publisher, except in the case of brief quotations embodied in critical reviews and certain other noncommercial uses permitted by copyright law. For permission requests, write to the publisher, addressed "Attention: Permissions Coordinator," at the address above.

Scripture is taken from GOD'S WORD®, © 1995 God's Word to the Nations.
Used by permission of Baker Publishing Group.

ISBN 978-0-9904939-0-7 (hardcover)
ISBN 978-0-9904939-8-3 (paperback)

Printed in the United States of America
First Printing, 2015

A colorful children's story infused with biblical declarations and positive affirmations

I Am Who God Says That I Am

Teaching Young Children Who They Are in God

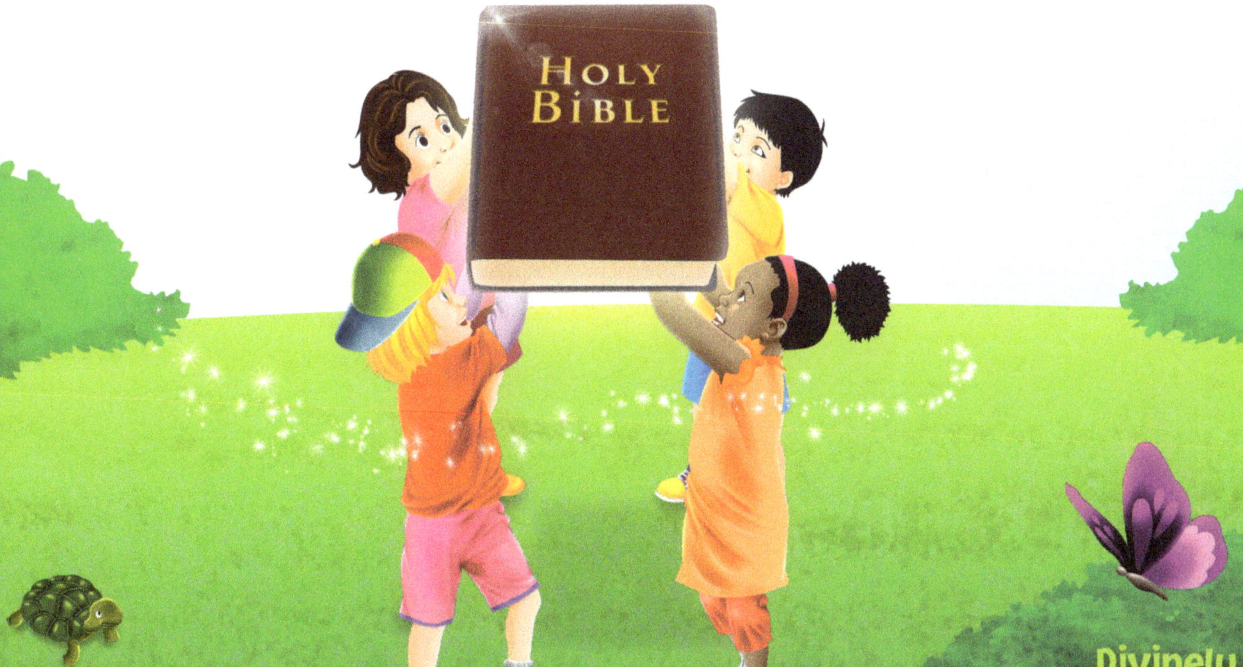

Divinely Inspired by
Terri L. Bell

Illustrated by Tea Seroya

Hello and welcome to the first book in the
Kingdom Kids "Speak Life" Declaration Series.

We are "Kingdom Kids"!

Did you know that you were made just like God
and He has something special for you to do one day?
Did you know that God loves you and you are his child too?
In Psalms 139, God says He knows you
and you are amazingly and miraculously made.
Wow, how awesome is that?

We want to invite you to read along with us,
as we share God's love with you.

We want to also say thank you to the parents and adults
who will be reading this book with you and sharing in this
divinely inspired opportunity to "Speak" and "Declare"
God's word into your life.

Let the journey begin...

I am special; God knows me.

I am made by God, He really loves me!

You are a holy people, who belong to the Lord your God.
He chose you to be his own special possession
out of all the nations on earth.
Deuteronomy 7:6

How precious are your thoughts concerning me, O God!
How vast in number they are!
Psalms 139:17

I am as happy as I can be.

I am special.

Be happy with the Lord, and he will give you the desires of your heart.
Psalm 37:4

He gave himself for us to set us free from every sin and
to cleanse us so that we can be his special people
who are enthusiastic about doing good things.
Titus 2:14

God loves me from my head to my feet, and everything you see just like my mommy and daddy who take care of me.

I am special.

We have known and believed that God loves us. God is love.
Those who live in God's love live in God, and God lives in them.
1 John 4:16

Train a child in the way he should go,
and even when he is old he will not turn away from it.
Proverbs 22:6

God loves me like the pretty butterflies way up high,

and the colors of the rainbow in the sky.

³ When I look at your heavens, the creation of your fingers,
the moon and the stars that you have set in place—
⁴ what is a mortal that you remember him
or the Son of Man that you take care of him?
Psalm 8:3–4

I am made by God and that is why I am special.

¹Oh Lord you have examined me, and you know me.
²You alone know when I sit down and when I get up.
You read my thoughts from far away.
Psalm 139:1–2

¹³You alone have created my inner being.
You knitted me together inside my mother.
¹⁴I will give thanks to you because I have been so amazingly and miraculously made.
Psalm 139:13–14a

God loves me like the big tall branches on a tree.

I am very brave, just look at me.

Consider this: The Father has given us his love.
He loves us so much that we are actually called God's dear children.
And that's what we are.
1 John 3:1a

Do not be afraid, because I have reclaimed you.
I have called you by name; you are mine.
Isaiah 43:1b

I am never afraid of anything.

I am special!

Look! God is my Savior.
I am confident and unafraid, because the Lord is my strength and my song.
He is my Savior.
Isaiah 12:2

"I have commanded you,
'Be strong and courageous! Don't tremble or be terrified,
because the Lord your God is with you wherever you go.'"
Joshua 1:9

I am very smart; just watch and see!

There is no one on earth the same as me.

I am special.

God gives wisdom, knowledge, and joy to anyone who pleases him.
Ecclesiastes 2:26a

Today the Lord has declared that you are his people, his own special possession, as he told you. But you must be sure to obey his commands.
Deuteronomy 26:18

God made
my two little hands and
my small round nose;

He made my beautiful eyes
and my ten tiny toes.

I am special.

God has made us what we are. He has created us in Christ Jesus
to live lives filled with good works that he has prepared for us to do.
Ephesians 2:10

You are people who are holy to the Lord your God. Out of all the people who live
on earth, the Lord has chosen you to be his own special possession.
Deuteronomy 14:2

Just like the flowers that grow, I am growing, too.

I am made by God and so are you!

But grow in the good will and knowledge of our Lord and Savior Jesus Christ. Glory belongs to him now and for that eternal day! Amen.
2 Peter 3:18

"Our Lord and God, you deserve to receive glory, honor, and power because you created everything. Everything came into existence and was created because of your will."
Revelation 4:11

Yes, I am special,
and God loves me.

I can do anything
if I only believe!

God loved the world this way: He gave his only Son so that everyone who believes in him will not die but will have eternal life.
John 3:16

I can do everything through Christ who strengthens me.
Philippians 4:13

I am who God says that I am.

The Spirit himself testifies with our spirit
that we are God's children.
Romans 8:16

The heavens were made by the word of the Lord
and all the stars by the breath of his mouth.
Psalm 33:6

Kingdom Kids Prayer

Dear God, my Lord and King
You are my every thing

You made me to look like you
You care about the things I do

You asked me to follow you
and that is what I am going to do

Thank you for the mom and dad you gave to me
and all those who love and take care of me

I am a Kingdom Kid because you made me
I am everything you said I would be

I am special to you and you are special to me
Thank you God for loving me

Now I will love everyone I see
So they can be a Kingdom Kid like me

In Jesus' name I pray, Amen!

Kingdom Kids Declarations

I am LOVED

I am CHOSEN

I am BRAVE

I am SMART

I am STRONG

I am UNIQUE

I am BEAUTIFUL

Proverbs 18:21a says that "death and life are in the power of the tongue"

Exercise: Have your child(ren) call these declarations out loud.
This exercise is sure to "Speak Life" and aid in building self-esteem, identity and purpose.

www.ingramcontent.com/pod-product-compliance
Lightning Source LLC
Chambersburg PA
CBHW061817290426
44110CB00026B/2900